BLEED CONTROL

SPECIALIST

Laura J. Kendall, MICP (RET), CPC.

We have online training in active shooter response & tactical bleed control that you can join anytime at www.traintorespond.com

Basic Emergency Treatment for Severe Arterial Bleeding

Call out for help!

Tell them to call 911 or your country specific emergency number!

Apply medical gloves or something to protect you from blood.

Perform an **RTA** to find life threatening bleeding.

Arterial Bleed? - YES! - begin self aid or victim aid by applying **Direct Pressure** to the bleeding site.

Bleeding does not stop with direct pressure?

Immediately apply a Tourniquet (extremity only) and continue holding direct pressure on the wound.

Keep the victim supine, calm & warm.

Monitor the bleeding site.

Call 911 or your country specific emergency number!

Important Numbers

Emergency Services - call 911 or your country specific emergency number.

Local Police Department:_____.

Local Fire Department:_____.

Local Ambulance Squad:_____.

Workplace Information

Security Department:_____.

Facility Address:_____.

In a critical situation know the following:

Your location: _____.

Number you are calling from:_____.

Your cell phone/ call back number_____.

Content

Definitions

Bleed Control Specialist: A family or community member who recognizes a bleeding injury and acts to save lives.

EMS: Emergency Medical Services.

LE: Law Enforcement.

LEO: Law Enforcement Officer.

GSW: Gunshot Wound.

Cold Zone: An area where no significant danger/threat is reasonably anticipated.

Hot Zone: Ground zero - where the active killing is taking place.

RTA: Rapid Trauma Assessment.

Soft Target: A person or place unprotected/unarmored and vulnerable.

Staging area: A safe area which provides cover and concealment for responders, before they enter the scene.

Warm zone: An area close to the shooting, which is not completely secure and where you have a chance of being shot.

Tactical Trauma Care: A specific set of action steps utilized to provide immediate treatment of traumatically injured victims.

Triage: The act of sorting victims according to the seriousness of their injuries and from this treatment and transportation decisions are made.

Dedication

This book is dedicated to you, because you are taking the proactive and much needed stance of learning what to do during active threat situations and how to save lives using basic bleeding care and equipment.

Having knowledge and action steps to take during a critical incident may well save lives.

Acknowledgements

I would like to acknowledge the following agencies and sites for their invaluable wealth of information on active shootings, workplace violence and treating the wounded. Please take time to go to their websites and read the information as well as watch the videos.

The Department of Homeland Security.

FEMA.

Texas State University - Avoid Deny Defend.

The U.S. Department of Labor.

Ready Houston - Run Hide Fight.

OSHA.

Officer Survival Solutions.

North American Rescue.

Rapid Application Tourniquets.

TECC Guidelines (Current 2015)

National Safety Council.

Foreword

I've been in the field of EMS since 1981 and a NJ mobile intensive care paramedic since 1986, retiring from the street in 2018. Not in a million years did I envision the violent and hate filled world we live in today. Now more than ever, it is important to educate yourself on how to survive an active killing, act of workplace violence or terrorist attack and how to provide basic emergency first aid to the wounded.

Active threats aren't going away and I believe it is time to arm ourselves with the knowledge and action steps, we need in order to keep ourselves alive and safe, should we be caught in such an event. Learning to recognize, react, survive, and aid the wounded during such an event or even during a medical or traumatic emergency may well be the best gift you will ever give yourself, your family and community.

Laura J. Kendall, MICP (RET), CPC

Founder / Owner: Train To Respond, LLC

Other books by Laura J. Kendall

(Available on amazon.com & barnesandnoble.com)

1. Active Shooter Response Training Manual for EMS, Police & Fire.

2. Active Killer Survival Manual for Civilians

3. Active Shooter Response & Tactical Trauma Care for Family, Community and Business.

Live Training & Education Courses

OSRT: Officer Shot Response Training Course for Professional First Responders.

ASRT: Active Shooter Response Training Course for Professional First Responders.

ASRT/TBC: Active Shooter Response & Survival Training - Tactical Bleeding Control for Civilians.

Join our online training at www.traintorespond.com

Module One

Bleeding

Remember to protect yourself against blood borne diseases if possible by wearing medical gloves or a sealed protective barrier over your skin.

Three types of bleeding:

Capillary Bleeding

Smallest blood vessels that deliver oxygenated blood to the tissues and take back deoxygenated blood to the veins. Capillary bleeding is slow and oozes out. It stops quickly with direct pressure.

Venous Bleeding

Veins carry blood with little to no oxygen in them which explains the dark red color. They are not under pressure and bleed slow and steadily.

Deep cuts have the potential to cut open veins.

The best way to stop most cases of venous bleeding is to put direct pressure on the wound.

This is when a Pressure Bandage would be applied to help slow and stop the bleeding.

But remember we are not stopping the pulse in the affected area so not too tight!

Arterial Bleeding – the deadly killer!

Arteries carry freshly oxygenated blood (which is why arteries have bright red blood in them) from the heart to be distributed to the tissues of the body. Because they carry rich oxygenated blood that must go throughout the body, they are under pressure. This is why arterial bleeds are so deadly.

Arterial bleeding is the least common but the most deadly type of bleeding. In an arterial bleed the blood **is bright red and spurts out each time the heart beats. Picture a garden hose on at full blast. This is what a bleed of a major artery looks like. Literally the victim will be dead in 3 - 5 minutes if no first aid is given.**

In most cases of arterial bleeding, direct and extremely firm pressure on the wound is the best way of stopping it.

If direct pressure is not applied, a severe arterial wound can cause you to bleed to death within a few minutes.

Arterial bleeding may be hard to notice right away if the victim is wearing dark clothing or if it's a dark environment. You will need to look at the clothing and watch for pooling of blood in one spot that seeps through the clothing.

<u>Treat fast - you can bleed out in 3-5 minutes!</u>

<u>If you have attempted to control the bleeding with direct pressure and it will not stop, you must immediately apply a tourniquet to stop the bleeding.</u>

<u>Here are some things to remember:</u>

1. Tourniquets are for massive bleeding and control.

2. Never apply a tourniquet over a wound.

3. Only use them on extremities.

4. Write down the time of application for EMS/Hospital.

5. Once applied it stays on - DO NOT REMOVE.

<u>Tourniquets should be used to control massive bleeding that cannot be stopped with direct pressure.</u>

The benefit of tourniquet use in patients with massive hemorrhage has been proven and is now the standard of care.

Module Two

Tourniquets

If direct pressure does not stop the bleeding quickly then immediately apply a tourniquet!

There is a shift from old thinking (in cases of massive bleeding) of tourniquet as a last resort.

Evidence is supporting tourniquets save lives from treatable exsanguination injuries.

Self Aid - treating yourself.

Buddy Aid – treating a victim

Tourniquet Do's & Don'ts

Remember Tourniquets are for extremities ONLY

1.Place the tourniquet above the affected joint. Never over top of a joint! (Joints in the arm are the wrist, elbow, shoulder. Joints in the leg are ankle, knee, hip.)

2. High & Tight! Apply the tourniquet 3 - 6 inches above the wound and never over top of the wound!

3. Tighten until bleeding stops and there is no distal pulse.

4. Tell EMS or the hospital there is a tourniquet on the victim you are with.

Types of Tourniquets

CAT - Combat Application Tourniquet

A CAT is a truly effective tool that when used correctly stops bleeding in extremities. The CAT is patented and can be applied using one hand.

Image courtesy of North American Rescue

To learn more go to North American Rescue

https://www.narescue.com/

To join our online Bleed Control Specialist Training go to traintorespond.mykajabi.com

RAT - Rapid Application Tourniquet

Rats Medical defines the RAT as: ☐R.A.T.S – *Rapid Application Tourniquet* – A solid vulcanized rubber core with a nylon sheath combined with a unique locking mechanism make this a simple and incredibly fast *tourniquet* to *apply* to self or others. The RATS hallmark is use under stress.

U.S. PAT. NO. 9,168,044

Image courtesy of Rats Medical

To learn more go to Rat's Medical

https://ratsmedical.com/

Using a Swat T tourniquet step by step

Deploy SWAT-T Tourniquet and Stretch it tight. Wrap it 6 inches above the wound if possible.

Continue the wrapping process to ensure tightness with each wrap.

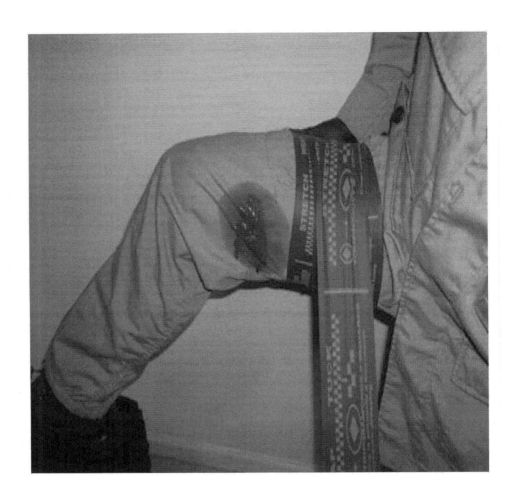

As you come to the last few inches, tuck the end of the tourniquet inside the wrap to secure it.

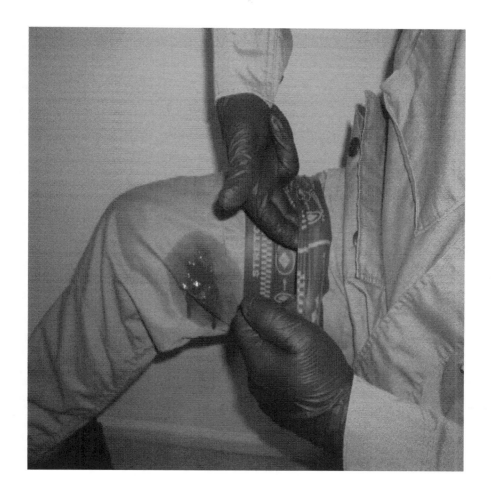

SWT: Stretch, Wrap and Tuck Tourniquet.

Images source: Officer Survival Solutions.

RECAP of Tourniquet Do's & Don'ts

Remember Tourniquets are for extremities ONLY

1.Place the tourniquet above the affected joint. Never over top of a joint!

2. High & Tight! Apply the tourniquet 3 - 6 inches above the wound and never over top of the wound!

3. Tighten until bleeding stops and there is no distal pulse.

4. Tell EMS or the hospital there is a tourniquet on the victim you are with.

Module Three

Pressure Bandages

Pressure bandages are used to control venous bleeding that is able to be slowed or stopped using direct pressure.

To use a pressure bandage:

Continue Holding Direct Pressure

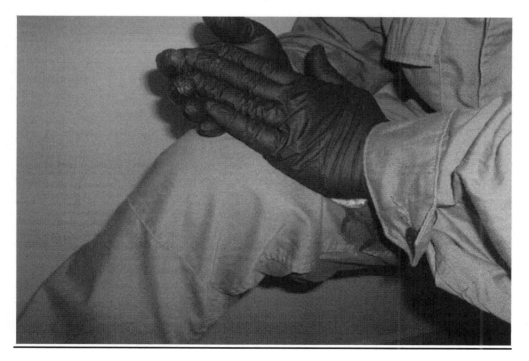

Deploy Emergency Pressure Bandage with non-stick pad directly over the wound

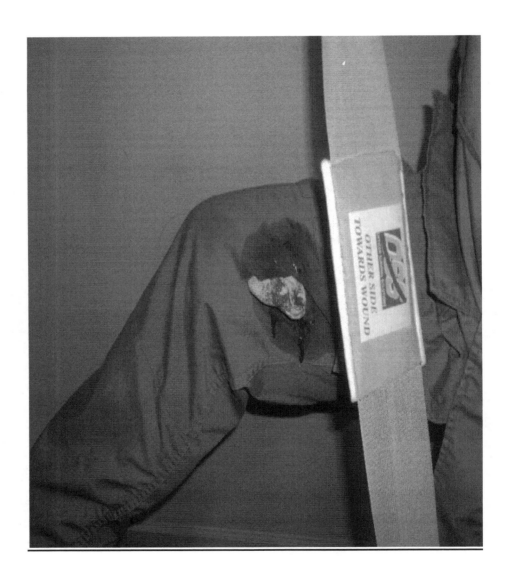

Wrap tightly creating pressure to be forced down onto the wound.

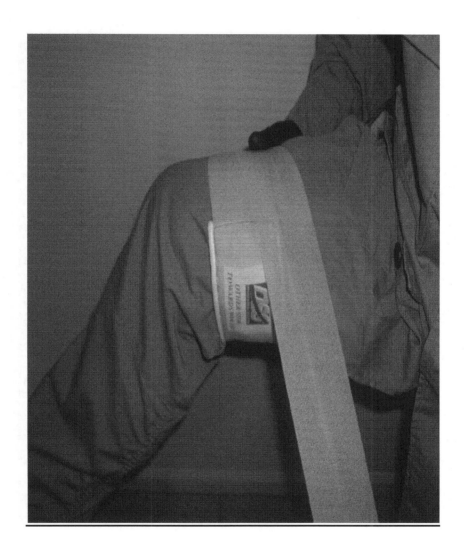

Wrap an inch below the wound and an inch above the wound

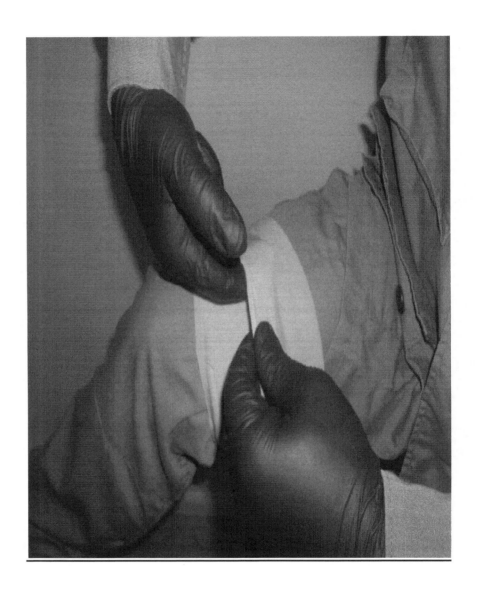

Secure by affixing the end onto the wrap

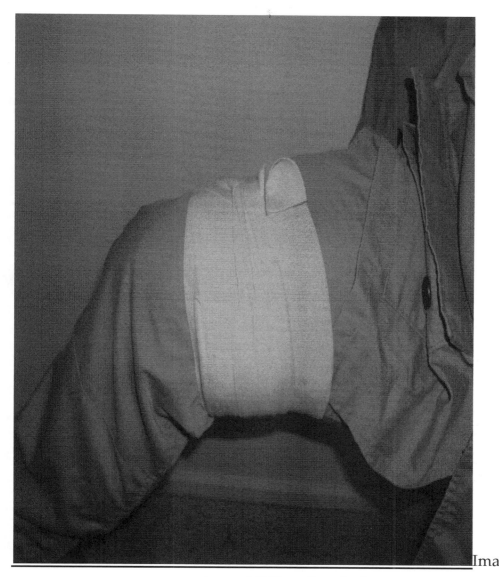

Module Four

Active Threat Survival

The purpose of this book and our training is to not only know how to stop bleeding, but to help give you the knowledge and action steps to be able to recognize that a violent event is happening, to be able to react quickly and appropriately to increase chance of survival.

Imagine suddenly hearing shots ring out! Would you know what to do? Would you delay acting because you are in denial an active shooting or terrorist event is happening?

God forbid you are shot, stabbed or caught in a blast. Would you know how to save your own life? Lately it seems people can be enjoying a regular day when suddenly mayhem breaks loose as an active killer starts murdering people before their eyes!

Would you know the steps to take to increase your chance of survival if you suddenly found yourself in such an attack?

What is an Active Killer / Shooter

Homeland Security describes an Active Shooter/Killer as an individual actively engaged in killing or attempting to kill people in a confined and populated area. In most cases, Active Killers use firearms and there is no pattern or method to their selection of victims. Active Killer situations are unpredictable and evolve quickly.

The FBI definition of a mass shooting requires four or more people killed in one instance (not including the perpetrator.)

This leaves out the multitude of other shootings where multiple people are injured or killed, but four or more people are not killed at one location

***Mass Shooting Tracker is a site from the GrC community, that tracks shootings involving both multiple individuals wounded & killed.

Mass Murderer

One assailant who kills at least 4 others in a 24 hour period.

• 1930 – 1960: Most active killers know their target or commit murder during a felony.

• 1960 – present: Most active killers go for soft targets and shoot unknown bystanders.

Active Threats

Active Threats come in many forms. They include active shooters, terrorists and workplace violence offenders.

Active Shooters

An active shooter is defined as an individual actively trying to kill or attempting to kill people in a confined and populated area.

-Most use firearms.

-No pattern to victim selection.

-Pick soft targets with limited security.

-They don't go in planning to survive. Most take their own life or are killed by law enforcement.

Active Shooter Profile

Described as:

-Social isolates.

- Harbor feelings of hate and anger.

- Often have had some contact with mental health professionals.

- FBI states very few have previous criminal records.

- Most have had some type of emotional hardship or loss.

Workplace Violence

Workplace violence is a complex and complicated issue and cannot be covered in-depth in this book. It is suggested that you read OSHA's Fact Sheet on Workplace Violence and The U.S. Department of Labor's Workplace Violence Program. The links for both can be found by going to www.traintorespond.com and clicking on the free resources tab.

According to OSHA'S 2002 Fact Sheet workplace violence is defined as:

Workplace violence is violence or the threat of violence against workers. It can occur at or outside the workplace and can range from threats and verbal abuse to physical assaults and homicide, one of the leading causes of job-related deaths. However it manifests itself, workplace violence is a growing concern for employers and employees nationwide.

➡Nothing can be an absolute guarantee that you will not become a victim of workplace violence, but knowing simple steps can decrease the possibility.

➡Employees should attend a personal safety training program that will educate them how to recognize, avoid or diffuse violent situations.

➡Always alert supervisors of any concerns for safety/security. Trust your gut and if you feel there is a danger take proper precautions.

Read The OSHA'S 2002 Fact Sheet workplace violence at

https://www.osha.gov/OshDoc/data_General_Facts/factsheet-workplace-violence.pdf

The U.S. Department of Labor's Workplace Violence Program classifies three levels of warning signs.

View the full program at https://www.dol.gov/oasam/hrc/policies/dol-workplace-violence-program.htm

Level One - Early warning behavioral signs a person may display.

- Intimidating or bullying .

- Discourteous/ disrespectful .

-Uncooperative.

-Verbally abusive.

Level Two - Escalation of the situation. If warranted call 911!

- Argues with co-workers, customers, vendors and management.

-Refuses to obey policies & procedures.

-Sabotages equipment/steals property.

-Verbalizes desire to hurt co-workers or management.

- See self as a victim and that management is against them.

<u>Level Three</u> - Dangerous escalation of the situation! Call 911!!

<u>Level Three Behavior</u>

-Intense anger.

-Suicidal threats.

-Physical fights.

- Destruction of property.

-Showing extreme rage.

-Use of weapons to hurt or harm others.

Remember

In all cases secure safety for yourself and others!

Call 911 if it is warranted or you feel you are in danger!!

Leave the area if you feel you are in danger.

Cooperate with responding law enforcement.

Notify your supervisor.

Document behaviors you observe.

Follow the policies and procedures set in place by the employer or corporation you work for.

It is highly suggested that you get more in-depth training and resources regarding workplace violence. This is a brief overview and does not encompass all the knowledge you need to know regarding workplace violence.

Domestic Violence

According to The U.S. Department of Labor's Workplace Violence Program there will be early warning signs of violence that is escalating outside the workplace.

A domestic violence victim may show symptoms such as:

-Increased fear, emotional episodes, physical injury.

-Work performance deterioration.

By recognizing and intervening when early warning signs are evident a more serious incident may be prevented.

***If a domestic abuser shows up at work with the intent of harming the victim or others this requires a Level Three response immediately.

Call 911 and secure safety for yourself and others!

Terrorism

Terrorist attacks are happening all over the world with alarming frequency.

Clearly the world has changed and we must be highly alert wherever we are to the possibility of an Active Killer or act of terrorism occurring.

Trust your gut instinct. If something feels off to you then react.

Hesitation and disbelief it is happening literally can kill you.

Surviving an Active Threat

One of the biggest keys to survival is recognizing that it is going down and you are caught in an Active Threat event.

He or she who hesitates is lost - literally!

All hope is not lost. There are some proven action steps you can take that can help you survive an active threat or shooting.

According to the U.S. Department of Homeland Security's Active Shooter - How To Respond and Ready Houston – Run Hide Fight, there are three things you can do if caught in an Active Killer situation.

1. Run!

Not running blindly, but with a plan!!

1. Know your route. Plan it ahead!

2. Leave your stuff behind. Stuff does not save lives!

3. Help others get out!

4. Stop others from heading towards the Active Killer!

5. Keep your arms in the air - like you are surrendering as you run out. This will help you and others exiting not get shot by responding law enforcement.

6. Follow the instructions of law enforcement.

2. Hide!

Cover vs. Concealment

In an Active Killer situation one of the things to think about is "what can I hide behind?" There are two types of places to consider.

Cover is an object or objects that are likely to stop bullets. This not only helps you from being seen, but also will protect you from bullets. Most obvious types of cover are cement walls, vehicles (engine area), steel doors etc…

Concealment is basically not being seen. Concealment offers no protection. Examples of concealment are sheetrock and plywood walls, desks, vehicle doors, tinted glass, and bushes, etc.

In an Active Killer situation it is important to know if you are using cover or concealment. An excellent mental exercise I do when in a building or a public place is to observe for areas of cover and concealment.

When selecting cover do note that the type of firearm used will make a difference in how much protection it will provide.

As we have seen in recent attacks in Dallas and other places; the use of large caliber, rapid fire firearms will penetrate objects as well as cause death and devastating injuries more than smaller caliber ones.

Having knowledge of where you are moving to before you leave is important as well. Have a plan before you start to move! This is why it is important to know your surroundings. Knowing which direction windows open and what level in a building you are in is extremely essential. This knowledge is also important to let first responders know where you are and what you are reporting!

3. Fight - last resort only!

Fighting as a last resort!

Historically Active Killers do not like confrontations. The new breed of terrorists however have the main purpose of killing and wounding as many as possible.

We are not advocating purposely putting yourself in harm's way, but sometimes there is no other choice but to defend yourself. You have a right to defend yourself!

Having some self defense skills before having to defend yourself is obvious. The time and money used to take basic martial arts training or pepper spray training can be a lifesaver.

Let me reiterate that you have a right to defend yourself if you are being attacked and your life is in danger.

Don't fight fair! Your attacker isn't fighting fair and wants you dead.

In my live and online training courses I focus mainly **on Avoid - Deny - Defend** as the way to survive an active shooting.

At the ALERRT Center in Texas State University they examined these choices(run, hide, fight) even further and found another way of reacting to an active killer situation.

They found three things you can do that have proven effective if caught in an Active Killer situation. What you do matters!!

You have 3 choices:

1. Avoid!

2. Deny!!

3. Defend!!!- You have a right to defend yourself!!

According to the ALERRT Center - Avoid - Deny - Defend the first step starts with your state of mind.

AVOID

1. Situational Awareness - be aware of what is going on around you.

2. Have an exit plan. (Know your exits not just the door you came into.)

3. Move away from the threat as quickly as possible.

4. The more distance and barriers between you and the threat or shooter increase survival.

DENY

When it is difficult or impossible to get away from the threat you must deny!

1. Keep distance between you and the threat/shooter.

2. Create barriers to prevent or slow down a threat /shooter from getting to you

3. Turn the lights off. and silence your phone or other devices.

4. Remain out of sight and quiet by hiding behind large objects.

5. Lock the doors.

6. Be ready to react if the threat gains entry.

DEFEND

If you can't get way for the threat/shooter or deny then you must be prepared to fight and defend yourself.

You have the right to survive!

I'll talk a little about mindset here. Mindset is everything in these type of attacks. You must have the mindset that "I AM GOING TO SURVIVE!"

1. Be aggressive and committed to your actions!

2. Don't fight fair!

3. You have the right to survive! You are fighting for your life!

You can learn more at avoiddenydefend.org

My personal thoughts and preparation to how I'd approach surviving an Active Threat or Shooting.

The number one tip I can offer is to trust your gut feeling. If something doesn't feel or seem right then do not enter the area or building. If already inside then take immediate action. Hesitation/disbelief can literally cost you your life!

Sadly in this new day and age of violence I view the world differently than I did growing up in the 1960's, 1970's and 1980's.

Now every time I go to a public place, business, shopping venue etc... I take a moment to ask myself the following: If I hear gunfire or see something that my gut tells me is wrong and an attack is impending what will I do?

Try this mental exercise next time you are out in a public place.

1. What is my best route of exit? Where is the closest exit?

2. If one exit is blocked by the attacker where are the others that I may run to?

You must run with a plan and know all the exits ahead of time. Running frantically and without a plan can get you killed.

3. I pay attention to my surroundings and the people around me.

Is anyone acting strangely that sets off my inner alarm bell?

Is there an odd package or back pack sitting by itself that may signal an explosive device?

4. If there is no way to get out then where can I take cover?

Remember Cover is something that will take a bullet for you(such as a cement wall) as well as hide you from the active killer.)

If I can't find cover then how will I hide to conceal myself from view of the active killer?

Remember: Concealment will not protect you and will only offer a hiding place.

Remember to silence your cell phone or anything that might alert the shooter to your location.

Remembering that concealment offers no protection, know that if there is an opportunity (the threat moves away from the area) for you to leave and exit or get to cover or safety, then take it.

If I am able to get into a room then how can I secure the door?

Does it open inward? Can it be lock? Can it be blocked with heavy objects?

If the door opens outward can it be secure by wrapping a belt around the upper metal hinge and prevent it from opening?

Are there any windows that open and allow exit?

Remember to shut off the lights and hide against the wall beside the secured door so that if the killer looks in he/she will not see you, but you will be able to react if they gain entry.

5. To the best of ability and not endangering myself I will try to alert, prevent others from entering the area or moving toward the killer or help them escape. I will not however let a person who will not move stop me from exiting.

6. When exiting keep hands and arms in the air! The cops don't know if you or I are good or bad! Keeping arms up in surrender will help you not get shot by responding law enforcement.

7. If law enforcement is not on the scene, call 911 or your local emergency number as soon as it is safe. If you call 911 inform them of the what is happening and do not hang up until they tell you to!

Remember when caught in an attack you and I are the eyes and ears of the responding law enforcement officers!!

8. Follow the instructions of law enforcement.

If you have to fight as a last resort then how will you do it?

What objects can you use to do a counter attack should it be your life or the attackers?

Are there any other people willing to help you?

Do not fight fair and use anything and everything can to take the attacker down. Your life depends on what you do!

Our mindsets must be that we will survive!

It has been found that lone active shooters do not like confrontations, however the new breed of terrorists have the main purpose of killing and wounding as many as possible.

I am absolutely not advocating purposely putting yourself in harm's way, but sometimes there is no other choice but to defend yourself.

Having some self defense skills before having to defend yourself is obvious. The time and money used to take basic martial arts training or pepper spray training can be a lifesaver.

Module Five

Hemostatic / Combat Gauze

Hemostatic Gauze is an chemical agent that stops bleeding. There are several different kinds. If you are EMS, Fire or Police remember: **It must be approved for use in your state and by your agency.**

Hemostatic Gauze is used when direct pressure and an applied tourniquet do not stop the hemorrhaging or the injury is in an area you cannot apply a tourniquet, such as the neck or shoulder, groin.

➡It is important to be trained in the use of hemostatic gauze and feel confident in your ability to use it properly and when needed.

Step 1: **Tear open Hemostatic Gauze pouch** at the indicated tear notches **and take out the Hemostatic Gauze.**

Step 2: Pack the Hemostatic Gauze all the way down into the wound cavity until you make contact with the severed or torn artery.

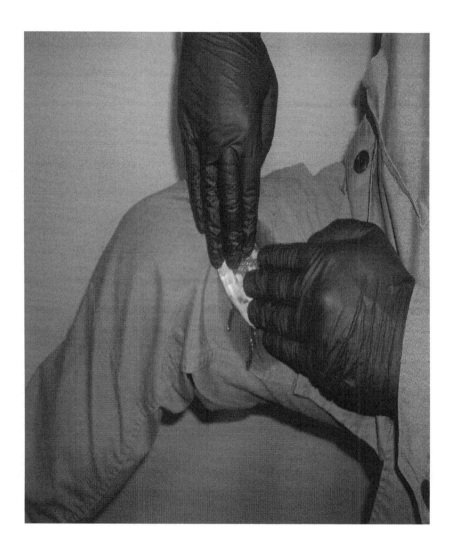

<u>Step 3</u>: Immediately apply direct pressure and hold that for at least <u>3 minutes.</u>

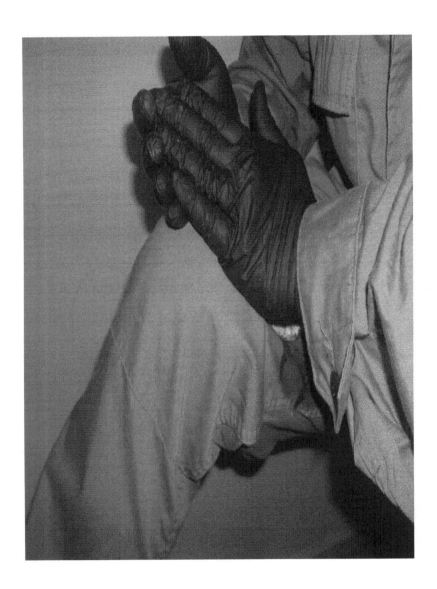

Applying the pressure bandage

Step 1: Apply the Emergency Pressure Bandage with non-stick pad directly over the wound.

Step 2: Wrap tightly creating pressure to be forced down onto the wound.

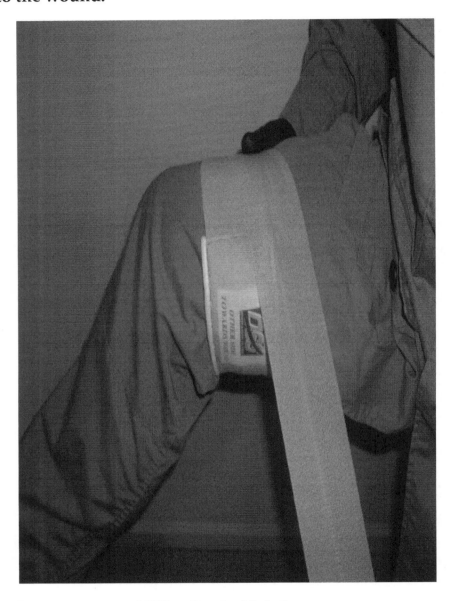

Images courtesy of Officer Survival Solutions

Pictures courtesy of Officer Survival Solutions

Module Six

Rapid Trauma Assessment

Positioning Your Victim

Now we will start digging deep into the aftermath of an active shooting. Here we will learn how you can help yourself or other victims of a shooting or penetrating traumatic injury such as a stabbing.

** If possible, whenever rendering emergency aid, wear medical gloves or some type of sealed protective barrier to protect you self from blood borne diseases.

Law Enforcement will enter the hot zone with the single goal of neutralizing the shooter. Once the shooter is neutralized they will aid victims. Until then you will be on your own and may be the first one to render aid to the victims or perform self aid.

This is rapidly changing, but right now most EMS providers are not trained or properly outfitted with ballistic gear to enter the hot zone or warm zone!

However if properly trained and outfitted with ballistic gear, emergency medical services may be directed into the warm zone (where there is a chance they could be shot) to help you, but most likely they will be in a staging area until the scene is declared safe by PD.

➡Be alert and follow law enforcement directions.

Bystander First Responders, the first question you need to ask yourself is; 'Is the scene safe?'

If the scene is not safe and you could be shot or killed, do not attempt rescue or treatment, unless trained specifically for such an event.

<u>Your safety comes first! Always!!</u>

<u>Rapid Trauma Assessment - RTA</u>

Remember to protect yourself from blood borne diseases as best as possible in these situations<u>.</u>

<u>Wearing medical gloves is best!</u>

When you come upon an injured or shot person, the first thing you will do is a rapid assessment for signs of life and for life threatening bleeding.

This assessment should take no more than 10 seconds.

Check: Are they conscious? Can they speak?

Check: Do they have a pulse? Are they breathing?

-Check wrist (radial artery) You will find this by pressing down with two fingers (not your thumb) in the groove on the thumb side of the wrist.

-If you can't feel the radial pulse then immediately check the neck (carotid artery).

Hint: feel for the carotid pulse by running your pointer & middle finger down the center of the throat and about midway down slide them towards you into the groove on the side of the neck. Press down to feel for a pulse.

CPR is not attempted in an area (hot zone or warm zone) that has not been declared safe and secured by police.

If the killer has been neutralized and the scene declared safe (Cold Zone) then if trained begin CPR.

If the victim has a pulse and is breathing then check for bleeding.

Triage

If there are multiple victims and not enough civilian rescuers, then triage must come into play.

As hard as it may be to do if there are more victims then rescuers you must move on to the one you can still try to save. One who is still alive, but may be bleeding out takes priority.

Positioning of victims

Because every situation is different and I can't be there with you I want to let you know about accepted patient positions to consider when deciding how to best position the victim during treatment.

National Safety Council First Aid training recommends the following:

Recovery Position

In an Active Killer Attack in the hot or warm zone place an unconscious, but breathing victim into the recovery position.

Recovery position is one in which you extend the victims arm above their head and then carefully roll the victim onto their side(same side as the extended arm) allowing the victim's head to be supported by the extended arm.

Bend both legs to help stabilize the victim in this position.

Open the victims mouth to allow drainage of blood and fluids.

Monitor their breathing.

Be ready to do CPR. (When doing CPR the victim must be on their back for you to do chest compressions and rescue breathing.)

<u>Shock Position</u>

Responsive victims with no evidence of trauma: you should position the person on their back and if it does not cause pain you may raise the victim's legs so the feet are 6 - 12 inches off the ground.

Unresponsive victim with no evidence of trauma: you should place the person in the recovery position.

Be ready to do CPR.

Spinal Motion Restriction

If your victim has a head injury or you suspect a spinal cord injury initiate the Spinal Motion Restriction position.

Responsive victim:

1. Explain that they need to hold their head still to prevent spinal movement.

2. Hold the victims head and neck with both hands in the position they are found to prevent movement of the neck and spine.

Unresponsive victim: Hold the victims head and neck with both hands in the position they are found to prevent movement of the neck and spine.

Open the airway with the Jaw Thrust Maneuver.

Continue to hold stabilization until help arrives. Monitor their breathing and be ready to do CPR

To learn CPR you can go to:

The National Safety Council http://www.nsc.org

The Red Cross http://www.redcross.org

The American Heart Association www.heart.org

.

Module Seven

Special Circumstances

Traumatic amputations

This can happen in a bombing or other massive traumatic event.

Traumatic amputations – control massive bleeding!

Do an RTA – find life threatening injuries or problems.

1. Apply direct pressure

2. If bleeding does not stop apply a tourniquet.

3. Treat for shock.

4. Recover the amputated part if possible.

Preserve the amputated part by wrapping the amputated part in sterile saline soaked gauze and place it in a watertight container or resalable plastic bag. Place the protected part in container with ice. Do not allow the damaged part to come in direct contact with ice.

In a blast injury the limb or parts may be too badly damaged to recover or preserve.

Impaled objects

Many explosive devices have been loaded with shrapnel which upon detonation will impale into the victims. Likewise ordinary objects caught up in the blast wave can impale themselves into victims.

Perform an RTA to find life threatening injuries or problems.

1. Treat life threatening problems or injuries immediately.

2. Leave impaled object in and stabilize it.

**The reason we leave impaled objects in is that the object itself may be what is sealing off the bleeding artery. To remove it would cause massive bleeding as well as further injury to organs.

3. If the object is large such as a fence it may require extrication/cutting.

4. Treat major bleeding.

Preparing for the arrival of the Professional First Responders

It is good to know the information the emergency responders will need to know upon their arrival.

Try to have the following pertinent information written down, to give to the emergency responders when they arrive.

1. Patient's full name.

2. Patient's age and date of birth.

3. Do not resuscitate order – legal document containing the patient's wishes in life threatening situations.

4. Patient's medical history.

5. Patient's medications. - have these written down clearly.

   **Do not hand the first responders a bag or box full of various medication bottles they have to search through as this can slow down care and departure from the scene.

6. Patient's allergies

7. What happened? Paint the arriving first responders a clear picture of what is wrong or what happened to the victim or yourself.

The emergency providers will start asking questions.

Be prepared to answer the same questions and other ones as higher level providers arrive and take over patient care.

The questions asked are in the quest to get a complete and detailed picture of the patient's condition.

A clear picture of what is wrong will assist the emergency responders in their treatment and decision making for the patient.

A good way to remember the basic information emergency responders need is the acronym is the word -

SAMPLE

S – Signs and Symptoms the patient is having or has had before help arrived.

A - Allergies the patient has.

M - Medications the patient is taking.

P - Pertinent medical history of the patient.

L - Last oral intake. This is very important if the patient is facing immediate surgery for their condition.

E - Events leading up to the current illness or injury. What happened before the emergency responders arrived?

Know Your Emergency System

In New Jersey where I practiced there is a tiered emergency response.

First Responders: Police officers, Firefighters, or First Aid personnel who provide oxygen and basic care until other responders arrive. Their initial interventions can mean life or death for the patient until more advanced emergency responders arrive.

Emergency Medical Technicians: A provider trained in basic life support. EMT's duties include – patient assessment, determining if advanced life support is needed, administering oxygen and some medications, spinal

immobilization, extrication, bandaging and splinting, bleeding control, and emergency vehicle operations. Many EMTs are unselfish volunteers who provide emergency care to their communities free of charge.

Paramedics: A provider trained in advanced life support. Paramedics are able to assess patients and determine their condition. They then provide advanced interventions.

Advanced interventions include - intravenous fluids, endotracheal intubation, medication administration, rapid sequence intubation using sedation and paralytics, chest needle decompression, intraosseous infusions, nebulizer treatments, emergency tracheotomies, 12 lead EKG interpretation, and emergency vehicle operations. Their quick thinking and critical decisions can mean the difference between the patient living or dying.

EMTs and Paramedics may drive ambulances, but gone are the days of being called an 'ambulance driver'.

It is important to know the certification level of the emergency providers in your area. Emergency training and level of care are not the same in each state. Know who is coming to help you!

Dispatch Centers

In New Jersey we have a comprehensive911 dispatch system.

 Most dispatchers are highly trained and are your life link when an emergency occurs. They are often overlooked in the chain of emergency care, but I for one believe they are the most important. Without that link to a trained dispatcher no help is coming!

Many dispatchers are trained to provide direction in medical/traumatic emergencies and can help talk you through providing the initial care.

It is important you stay calm, listen to the dispatcher, answer all questions and do not hang up until they tell you to!

Putting it all together

1. Have situational awareness at all times. Especially when you are in an area with a large number of people.

2. If you find yourself in an active threat or attack - **Do not run without a plan! Remember Avoid - Deny - Defend - Survive!**
Think ahead of time. How will you get out? Plan your route of evacuation before proceeding.

3. Follow all police directives.

4. When aiding the wounded, to the best of your ability, identify and treat life threatening injuries.

5. When safe evacuate the wounded to emergency medical services (**note that with formation of rescue task force teams - EMS may be able to come to you. Know what is being done in your area to train your

first responders) and give a full report to first responders, including your treatment and location of all tourniquets.

6.. If still in the active threat and it is safe to do so then call 911 or your country specific emergency number.

As a bystander first responder your objective is to help to the best of your ability by finding life threats, stopping the bleeding and following all police directives.

Trauma Kits

There are many different types of trauma kits specifically designed for treating a severe arterial bleeding and gunshot/stabbing injuries. Consider these items when putting together an Active Killer/trauma kit.

1. Medical Gloves.

2. Tourniquet (Swat T, RAT, CAT).

3. Hemostatic Gauze.

4. Pressure Bandage.

5. Hyfin Chest Vented Seals - Two.

Each piece of equipment is vitally important in treating a severely injured victim. We will go over in depth how to utilize each piece of equipment in the Bleed Control Specialist Training Course.

Keeping a first aid kit on hand is a good idea. I keep one in my car and carry smaller ones in my purse and backpack.

It is important to cover any open cuts and bleeding wounds on yourself before providing care.

This is why you should have non latex medical gloves with you at all times.

I keep medical glove in my purse, car, and take them any place I go where I may have to help someone.

Using a trauma kit

The initial rapid trauma assessment of an injured victim will help you determine what is needed and how you will treat them.

Here are the companies I personally purchase my emergency equipment and training equipment from.

It is vital you purchase from a reputable companies as there have been fake tourniquets and equipment put out there by not so reputable companies.

I recommend the following and do not receive any compensation for doing so. They are truly the ones I have purchased from and had a great experience with.

1. North American Rescue -

https://www.narescue.com/

2. Officer Survival Solutions

- www.officersurvivalsolutions.com

3. Rat's Medical

https://ratsmedical.com/

4. Ready Man

https://www.readyman.com

I have also purchased equipment from amazon.com, but please make sure you know the listed company is the genuine thing before you purchase.

To enroll in our online training - Bleed Control Specialist go to traintorespond.mykajabi.com

Conclusion

Thank you for investing in yourself, your family, friends, co-workers and the future of our world.

Together we can make a difference and empower ourselves and others when confronted with acts of violence and terrorism

Remember to always be aware of your surroundings, if you see something or your gut tells you something is wrong do not enter the area and say something to the proper authorities.

To be better prepared it is imperative you get reputable online training or in person Active Threat Response Training and Tactical Trauma Care with live scenarios so you will feel better able to handle the critical situations mentioned in this book. Training is everything!

Online training is available at www.traintorespond.com

Most people don't know how to survive a shooting or active threat, and that costs lives. Our training can help.

Please remember to be aware of your surroundings at all times, know your exits always and if you see something - say something.

Be safe. Peace.

Laura J. Kendall, MICP (RET), CPC

email: laura@traintorespond.com

Find out more about our online training by visiting us www.traintorespond.com

Training for an Active Threat Event

If vs. WHEN

You must approach your preparation and training for active threat or shooter situations, not from a passive; "If position," but from the position of "WHEN."

Make training worse than real.

It has been said that: "You do not rise to the occasion in combat, you sink to the level of training."

It is quickly becoming the standard of care/training to provide Active Threat Survival & Bleed Control Training families, communities, businesses, groups, entertainment venues, schools and places of worship.

Any place that is a soft target or has large groups of people need to prepare and train for Active Threats.

Has your family, business, group, church, venue, range, club or community members been trained on how to react to survive should an active shooter or terrorist attack? Our training will give you and your people the skills and empowerment to step up and save lives.

***We offer live training workshops, lectures and classes in Active Threat Survival Training - Tactical Trauma Care.

Our training is available for families, communities, business, companies, groups, organizations, entertainment venues, places of worship, gun ranges & clubs and schools.

Contact us today at laura@traintorespond.com or our fastest response email is traintorespond@gmail.com

<u>Active Threat Survival Training & Bleed Control Training for families, communities and business.</u>

<u>We come to your location/s and are happy to travel across the United States to bring this vital knowledge and skill set to your people!</u>

Please contact us today to schedule a training course or request a speaker for your event.

Join our online training at traintorespond.mykajabi.com

Resources

FEMA Is - 907 - Active Killer: What you can do.
https://emilms.fema.gov/IS907/ASo1.

OSHA'S Workplace Violence Fact Sheet - https://www.osha.gov/OshDoc/data_General_Facts/factsheet-workplace-violence.pdf

Department of Labor's Workplace Violence Program- https://www.osha.gov/SLTC/workplaceviolence/

Ready Houston - Run - Hide - Fight - Surviving an Active Killer event.

Avoid Deny Defend - at www.avoiddenydefend.org

National Safety Council First Aid, CPR & AED Classes.

Our bleeding control training follows the recommendations of the TCCC - Tactical Combat Casualty Care and TECC - Tactical Emergency Casualty Care.

Works cited

1. Homeland Security - Office of Health Affairs - June 2015 First Responder Guide for Improving Survivability in Improvised Explosive Device and/or Active Killer Incidents.

2. Homeland Security - Active Killer Preparedness. www.dhs.gov/active-shooter-preparedness

3. Mass Shooting Tracker - This site counts the number of people shot rather than only the number killed and is updated as shootings happen. www.shootingtracker.com

4. Global Research - Mass Shootings in America: A Historical Review.

5. Ready Houston - Run Hide Fight!

6. Avoid Deny Defend from Texas State University ALERRT Center.

7. U.S. Department of Labor's Workplace Violence Program.

8. OSHA'S Workplace Violence Fact Sheet.

9. National Safety Council First Aid Quick Guide & workbook.

10. Pictures courtesy of Officer Survival Solutions.

Notes

44475222R00057

Made in the USA
Middletown, DE
07 May 2019